Prolific

Timothy Prolific Veit Jones

Rebel Waters
Brooklyn | Long Island

Published by Rebel Waters Ink (formerly Andre Maurice Press LLC)
Book Layout & Cover Design: Timothy Prolific Veit Jones

Photography: Manauvaskar Kublall for Media Sutra, Inc.
www.mediasutra.net

ISBN-13: 978-0-9779623-1-0
ISBN: 0-9779623-1-8
Library of Congress Control Number: 2006907272

For booking & all other inquires, contact tim@projones.com

Table of Contents

Acknowledgements

First and foremost, I would like to thank The Most High for blessing me with the ability to move people with my words. I would also like to thank my ancestors and deceased loved ones for guiding me to create in their spirit.

I am indebted to many for their continued support, love, and advice. I'd especially like to thank my parents, my grandparents, aunts, uncles, and extended family for always supporting my unusual path, nature, and approach to life.

My artistic journey is the result of many friendships, collaborations, conversations, college classes, Bible studies, church services, and community organizing. I'd like to thank all of my professors, pastors, comrades, and fellow artists for all they have taught me.

Publisher's Note

Peace & Blessings! Welcome to the inaugural release of the newly restructured André Maurice Press, LLC. We've come a long way since my chapbook, *Explosion of a Dream Deferred.* Consider this chapbook a herald of what's to come. We have one artist signed, and several in negotiation to join our roster.

I'm sure some of you are wondering, "who is André Maurice?" André Maurice Veit was my first cousin. Among other things, André was a very bright, talented child who had a love for the arts. He was a trained tap dancer and pianist. The two of us were inseparable during family gatherings, whether it meant playing basketball, piano, or performing for our family dressed like our favorite singers and rappers. He passed away at the age of 12 saving the life of one of his friends. As a 12 year old myself, coping with his death was very difficult, and within a few years I found myself drifting away from piano toward acting and poetry as a catharsis.

In 2002, upon returning to Long Island, transferring from Cornell University to Hunter College, I met four young men that I eventually cofounded a group with called The Cataclysm. We were a group of poets & emcees, and experimented with fusing spoken-word and hip-hop. It was through this experience and my becoming a regular on the NYC open mic and slam circuit that the idea of releasing a book of poetry emerged. When I made the decision to self-publish, following in the footsteps of Jessica Care Moore, Haki Mahtibuti, Nikki Giovanni, Walt Whitman, and coutless other writers, I decided to name my self-publishing imprint after André. After printing my own book, I was inspired by my affiliation with Blackout Arts Collective to give others the opportunity to fulfill their dreams of releasing a book and capitalizing on their artistry. I decided that his name must live on in more than my own endeavors.

The mission of André Maurice Press is to provide an outlet for the published voices of the hip-hop generation. We are dedicated to cultivating talent, and providing writers a means through which to transform their expression into a form of economic empowerment. We believe that the ability to create is a blessing, and that we are vessels given the ability to touch souls through our craft. We believe in encouraging and developing artistry and writing abilities of young people, and providing them instruction in how to use their art as source of revenue while remaining true to their community. We produce high-quality, unique publications that range from chapbooks to full length releases. We exist to bring deferred dreams into fruition.

Timothy W. Jones
CEO/Founder

Preface

Timothy
—from the Greek Timetheus, "Honoring God"

Prolific
— adj. ⁻ marked by abundant inventiveness or productivity

I must start by saying that to most of you, this is my first book, a first introduction to my artistry, opinions, and passions. For me, this is a culmination of seven years of self-definition. I first started performing my poetry during my last year of high school at Friends Academy in Locust Valley, NY. My debut performance of my first real poem, "Young Black Male" was recited at a diversity club function with a salt and pepper audience. It was after having several people approach me after reading a poem that described my struggles with racial profiling, and my reaction to the epidemic of young black men being murdered by the police, that I realized that my work represented more than my own experiences and opinions. I continued to perform at talent shows, protests, and events at Cornell University, where I became a poet in demand for functions in the melanin enriched community.

When I transferred to Hunter College, I started reading my poetry at Bar 13's "A Little bit Louder" Monday night poetry series in 2001. At the time that I cofounded The Cataclysm, I had started to navigate the multitude of New York City poetry venues. For a period of several months, I went through a stage name identity crisis as I attempted to define and present myself in a manner that shielded my vulnerabilities, and would allow for personal growth.

Additionally, I was a member of a group full of people who were not using their actual names. After a discussion with my mother, I decided upon calling myself Prolific. It was a name that I lived up to considering the abundant quantity of poems that I wrote from 2001-2003.

The Prolific chapter of my life has come to a close, at least for now. I am more than capable of living up to the meaning of my given name, Timothy, and my next challenge is to write from a more personal space. My first chapbook, *Explosion of A Dream Deferred*, was a trumpet blown resounding with my reactions and observations of the world around me. It was highly influenced by my touring and organizing with Blackout Arts Collective, and printed a few months after the annual Lyrics on Lockdown tour. The focus of the tour is to raise awareness about the disproportionate incarceration of people of color in the United States, and the profit that many major corporations make from our imprisonment. Since slavery, we have remained a consistent source of cheap labor, and the plantation has been reincarnated in the form of the modern private prison. I was young, angry, and determined to take on the white supremacist power structure in this country with my poems as a tool for the upliftment and organization of my people.

My second manuscript, *Soul Eyes*, was an outlet for all the poems that would not fit the theme of *Explosion*. These were romantic and erotic poems. Contrary to common knowledge, I have a larger library of poems written for and about my interactions with women than anything else. I also possess a deep love of jazz music, and a knowledge of it's origins. The title is taken from the name of my favorite ballad played by celebrated saxophonist John Coltrane. If you are unfamiliar with his recordings, I suggest you listen to any of the following three albums as an introduction to his work: *The Ultimate Blue Train, A Love Supreme,* and *The Gentle Side of John Coltrane.* The book was highly inspired by one of my muses, and after things did not work out between us, I scrapped the book project and took a simultaneous break from performing and organizing.

The time that I spent away from actively practicing my art I used to solidify my adult life, and eventually craft a new vision for André Maurice Press. This vision was realized upon signing my first artist, Peuo Tuy. The journey to publishing her debut release is what inspired me to revise, compile, and reconfigure my work into the book that you are holding.

If you personally have any questions or comments about the poems, feel free to e-mail them to the address listed at the end of this preface. My work is written and will always be written to encourage critical thinking and dialogue.

And now, with no further adieu, I present to you my early writings. I give all thanks and praise to God for my gift, and for anything that I have written that may touch someone or bring them light; the imperfections belong to me alone.

Timothy William Veit Jones
Prolific
tim@projones.com

Explosion

of A

Dream Deferred

Libation

in the beginning

        was the   Word

and the   Word was   with God

and the

      Word

           was

                God

   when the word was spoken

poetry became   more

     than just another **token**

art form

        adorning   a

          dead white man's

                  epitaph

Samsara

in a dream state
i half-awake
a confused Avatar

i am
a konfined Krishna
a clandestine Christ
not blind but covering my eyes
internalizing malignant lies

i hear the Devil laugh
'cause i fear to say
my own name in vain
since i fear my own wrath

the crucifix is my stage
in consecrated wine i bathe
communion wafers are soap
incense my dope
praying to myself i choke
in fate's cruelest joke
i find my neck
is bound by the yoke

the chains, bracelets
platinum, diamonds,
and gold,
the music, videos,
fame, and hoes

its funny, while amassing riches
i sold my soul to place myself in chains
i cry to myself,
a god derranged

nominally emanicpated only to be reconstructed
so the slave master could mind fuck me
i'd flee only if the police would uncuff me
i pray to Paul Cuffee, Fred Hampton & Huey P
Sojurner, Harriet, & Ida B.,
invoke trinities of my ancestry

Shiva & Ogun
were force-fed PCP & told
to Pass the Courvoisier
they've drugged the gods
shipped them in crates
across the Atlantic & the United States
taught them to pick cotton
they give the gatherer pay
call it an offering of spite
little does the Black man know
he's spending his own life
selling his essence
distilled in crack pipes
dazzled by the bright lights
fame fortune & glory
not paying attention to history
not paying attention to herstory
forgetting Africa
before the colonizer
forgetting faith in God

before the baptizer
forgetting the elders' words
self-love can't be replaced
i'm held captive by mistakes

colonialism led me
to follow the wrong man
my rivers are flooding with mayhem
why should I pray this white man
give a dam
he's just a man
i once was Amun
i've been conned
searching for solutions
to be deposited in my palms
instead of taking my fate
into my own hands

in a dream-state
i half awake
a confused Avatar
bound by my inability
to acknowledge
my inner divinity
i am
a konfined Krishna
a clandestine Christ
looking for a mirror
to reflect the light
so i can recognize my face

stranger fruit

back in 1902
I saw the straaaaannnnngest thing
a tree that grew niggers
branch by branch
niggers in all shapes and sizes
fat niggers skinny niggers
thick niggers thin niggers
tall niggers short niggers
little niggers big niggers
dark niggers light niggers white niggers
purple niggers blue niggers
kinky niggers Jew niggers
Christian niggers Muslim niggers
Indian niggers colored niggers
rich niggers poor niggers
whore niggers
Black niggers niggers niggers niggers niggers niggers
smart niggers dumb niggers
slave niggers free niggers

this year we've got
Ph. D niggers
preacher niggers teacher niggers
stand up niggers sit-in niggers
run-out niggers gun-out niggers
chain-rockin' niggers
hanging themselves
with platinum & diamonds
soiled with their own nigger blood
hip-hoping niggers blues niggers

soul niggers
sole nigger
niggers have
no soul
damn they can dance
& put on a minstrel show!

tell me—what kind of nigger are you?
are you a field nigger?
a house nigger?
are you nigger police?
or that
nigger freeze!
found on the hoods of expensive cars?
A Wall Street...?   *Nigger please.*

maybe you're a nigger
lashing out at what he hates
therefore you kill niggers
so white men don't have to
because all good niggers hate themselves

a nigger kills a nigger
with a nigger in the cross hairs
nigger finger, trigger finger,
black bullet = a nigger's redeemer
BLAOW!
Wow!   Niggers bleed just like us!
Kill each other like us!
Niggers are forever trying to be like us!

Hell, it's downright American to kill a nigger!
Have you killed yourself a nigger today?
Have you killed your nigger self today?
Today have you killed a nigger?

Niggers kill themselves
in the mirror daily
trying to be good Americans
with blonde weaves, blue eyes,
civilized language, and capitalist ideology,
22 inch rims and illiteracy
are still in this year
along with Timberland chukkas, and fitted caps
ready to sell each other out in a minute
just for massa greenback's pat on the ass

What is a nigger?

a nigger is a slave
with no history, no heritage,
no link to the origins of civilization
incapable of producing anything of worth
furthering human society
a nigger is an inferior
a nigger is a figment
of your imagination

African people
we need to kill
the definition
of what a nigger is
before it kills us

A Daughter's Lullaby

Rock a bye baby, rock a bye
Rock a bye baby, rock a bye

I was born to the lullabies of lighters
warming crack pipes
separated from daddy
mommy's a zombie
creating geological processes
in her body
bringing her close to death by fire
mommy left daddy
she couldn't smoke him
in his absence
she betrothed herself to the rock
consummating this union
with her husband's master
the devil
she rides his semen
her passport to hell

one day daddy one day
one day daddy one day

doesn't everybody's mommy open her legs
to consume rocks with me daughter watching?
one day daddy sent a social worker
she yelled silent words at mommy with her eyes
daddy doesn't have to pay child support anymore
to feed mommy's pipe
now I can live with him

& have a normal life

daddy one day daddy one day
I'll make you proud of me
daddy I'll make you proud
daddy I'm too tired to do my homework!
memorizing fractions and world history
doesn't overwrite my memories
I never told you what they did to me
don't hit me again daddy
mommy's crack used to slap me in the face
not your hand too

work harder
you're being a bad girl
do that again & I'll break your neck
get upstairs, you're not having dinner

And everybody wonders why
I'm sad skinny, lazy, tired,
smart but won't apply myself
my actions are magnetic
hit me again daddy
if I'm not bad I don't see you
grandpa drives me to school
grandma taught me how to read
auntie cooks for me
you work hard
still living with your parents
but I never see you
what does she give you that I don't

daddy one day daddy
I'll go out and give some man
what these women give to you
to keep you from me
one day daddy
one day
you'll be proud
of
me

Rock a bye baby, rock a bye
Rock a bye baby, rock a bye

brown hands

she has beautiful
brown hands

white children
feared her blackness
would rub off
on them like oil
so they refused to hold them
in kindergarten

when she was in the water
they wouldn't swim in the pool
they feared
her blackness
would envelop them
they believed blackness
would infect them
with some unclassified ugliness
a pestilence with no cure

 she cried blue tears
at their red words
wet with the blood
of her self-worth

she grew up
light skinned
her hair fought colonization
she hated it
she was told

she was ugly
her half Native cousins
were pretty
with perfectly straight hair

in high school
she was an outcast
she went from being
the only black girl
in an all white private school
to that "not black enough" girl
attending a black public school

she became
the 1st black woman
in her workplace
some shunned her
called her an unqualified
affirmative action hire
despite her two Master's Degrees
she learned to work twice as hard
for half the recognition
now her brown hands
reach to open doors
for others
to rise past
red words & glass ceilings

a poor reason to say no

She said No.
I said why not me?
She said light-skinned men
glow in the dark
& that scares her
She wants
a dark or brown brotha
so She can have
brown babies
I was flabbergasted
color complexes
tend to perplex me
it's the 21st century
I am failing
the reverse paper bag test
conversely She and her sistas
would stomp me to the ground
if I were opposed to dating
dark-skinned women
this is a paradox

Mistrial

They lynched Matthew Shepard
for the same reason they lynched James Byrd
blood shed in the image of Emit Till
dragged bodies and barbed wire
eyes hanging out of sockets
death by hate

there are too many Sakia Gunns
killed in the image of Anthony Biaz,
Amadou Diallo, & Timothy Stansbury

They trained Bin Laden
financed Saddam, the Shah,
Taliban, Batista, the Israeli Army,
traded with DeClerk & Apartheid South Africa,
deposed Amiri Baraka as New Jersey Poet Laureate
they executed the Rosenbergs,
dropped the A-bomb on Hiroshima & Nagasaki

They invented chemical weapons
when they sent Native Americans on the Trail of Tears
with smallpox infected blankets
hunted Geronimo & Crazy Horse
slaughtered women & children at Wounded Knee

They accused brown people of being terrorists
used Christ to enslave
after they nailed that brotha to the cross
blew the nose off the Sphinx
invented colonialism

raped women of color
warred with the Chinese over opium
secretly bombed Cambodia
assassinated Walter Rodney, Malcolm X,
Medger Evers, Martin Luther King Jr.,
Fred Hampton, Steve Biko,
Patrice Lumumba, Ron Brown,
attempted to murder Bob Marley
exiled Assata Shakur
framed the Panther 21
locked up Mumia, H. Rap Brown,
Leonard Peltier, Mutulu Shakur, Sundiata Acoli,
raided Critical Resistance in Brooklyn

they flooded the ghettos with crack & heroin
they knew what they were doing
look at Huey Newton & Gil Scot Heron
they placed liquor & guns on every corner
bought BET, manufactured Clarence Thomas,
Ward Connerly, & Condi Rice

They made Uncle Ben, Aunt Jemima,
the Cream of Wheat Man,
Mantan the Watermelon Man, Jim Crow,
Blackface & Minstrel Shows

they made air pollution & endangered species
and backed out of the Kyoto Treaty
created Patriot Acts and Departments of Homeland Security
that they can run unchecked and stamp out dissent
by calling it unpatriotic

they kill niggers and faggots
chinks and spics
use alchemy to convert us into uncle toms
they want us subdued & distracted
so we can lose everything
we haven't always had next to nothing

they kill our youngest & our brightest,
rewrite our history
defile our ancestors
molest our children
rape our
mothers
sisters
daughters
sons
brothers
fathers
praying we all die
so they can rule the world

they have gotten away with all this
because we let them
most of us do nothing more
than cry about it
when we see it on NBC & CNN

shame on us
we effortlessly blame the system
when blood is on our hands
stained indelible
by our paralysis

Cherub

You and I did not start off as the best of friends
our initial dislike for each other
was traded between punches
I can't remember why We fought
no memories of slick talk or insults
usually We'd swing first
and talk later
if We talked
the two youngest grandchildren
competing for God knows what
do little boys ever really need reasons
to tackle one another
and practice submission holds?

I grew up.

You never got to.

somewhere between borrowing toys and fighting
We realized that We actually liked each other
as all the months flew between visits
We discovered We missed each other
You lived in Maryland
I lived in New York
and there weren't enough holidays
or vacation days in our parents' schedules
to see each other every month

when We were 9
the times you'd did come up

We shared a little hip-hop
We'd run into the basement
on a quest for hand-me down jeans
5 sizes too big to wear backwards
and belts to fasten on the last loop
so that We could do our best mock Kriss Kross
performance for our family
by the time Hammer came out
We were devout followers
You'd ask to borrow my extra pair of Hammer pants
I don't think I ever got them back
Despite our outrageous love of MC Hammer
a 40+ man who danced around with women in coochie cutters
We always maintained that Vanilla Ice was whack
despite your brother's attempts to convince us otherwise

me, your brother, and your sister
would spend hours on piano
playing fur elise
harmonizing boyz ii men songs
We'd take day trips to Jones Beach
and eat at least 2 bags of seedless grapes
by the time your siblings came back from the water
there were none left

at the dinner table we'd fight
over the last olive or pickle
We'd settle to have it split in half
by a parent

Childhood is innocent.

I never knew you witnessed so much
I barely could deal with my parents divorcing at 17
You dealt with it at 10
I hope you didn't feel alone like I did
I didn't have any brothers or sisters
to share the pain with

I wish We could have talked more
We were too young to spend hours on the phone
I wish you could have grown up
We could have exchanged prom stories
critiqued Wu-Tang albums
marveled at how LL Cool J was STILL making hits
I wish I didn't have to struggle to remember your voice

You were just 12 years old
I know they say life ain't over till it's over
but You had barely begun to live
You gave your friend a gift
his life
in place of your own

I can never simply remember you
as just a child
not when You gave so selflessly
what many grown men
would be cowards to sacrifice

Harlem

What happens to a dream deferred?

Does it dry up
like a raisin in the sun
Or fester like a sore—

And then run?
Does it stink like rotten meat?
Or crust and sugar over—

Like a syrupy sweet?

Maybe it just sags
like a heavy load.

Or does it explode?

— Langston Hughes

Explosion of a Dream Deferred

i walk through halls
filled with the echoes
of deferred dreams
exploding

recognizing eyes *sagging*
due to the weight of the
heavy loads inside
the minds of folk whose souls choke
under the yoke of American injustice

i walk through halls
filled with the echoes
of deferred dreams
exploding

remembering brothers and sisters
whose dreams exploded
rocking the foundation
of white supremacy
they dared to dream while in hell
all they saw around them was fire
so they stole the light they found
delivering it to humanity like Prometheus
sustaining the life of the Third World
with the resource our toils
can cause us to lack   energy

the walls of the pen
caused many warriors to pick up the pen

their words like shanks were slowly sharpened
poised with purpose to pierce
the belly of the beast & bust it wide open

i walk through halls
filled with the echoes
of deferred dreams
exploding

i don't see
criminals behind bars
i see the dreams of children discounted
too many teachers and leaders
resemble the instructor
of a young Malcolm Little
who told him his desire to become a lawyer
was unrealistic for a nigger,
how many people
have heard those words
and ended up with their fingers on triggers
causing hammers to strike
propelling them to survive
they exercise the only form of entrepreneurship
available to them so they hustle

i walk through halls
filled with the echoes
of deferred dreams
exploding

i see youth
plucked from one war

on the streets
transplanted to another
behind bars

i see soldiers
plucked from one war
on the streets
transplanted to another
behind bars

other folks
see street niggas

i see brothers
i see sisters
i see leaders
emerging from the flames
of deferred dreams

so many
had a fire ignite
while in jail
think of Dr. King's Letter
from his Birmingham cell
think of a hustler named Detroit Red
transforming into Malcolm X
think of Nelson Mandela's will that wouldn't relent
think of Assata Shakur and her liberation
Frederick Douglass escaping the plantation
Patrice Lumumba's speeches after his incarceration
and Harriet Tubman's astronomical navigation

when will humanity learn
the simple lesson
Langston Hughes tried to teach us

although deferred dreams
may *sag like a heavy load*
when contained like volatile chemicals
they *explode*
and when that explosion is harnessed
it becomes
the greatest
catalyst
for change

Soul Eyes

we should just be dancing

You are far from perfect
I am far from apostolic
like the functional alcoholic
I sit at work
contemplating when I'll taste you next
we are teetering on liminality
afraid that letting go of our inhibitions
will make us fall
from the safety of our hang-ups
breaking the see-saw
balancing our connectedness

You, afraid to let go of the past
I, afraid to show my hand
flashing my flush could make you fold
both of us are over concerned
with concepts of control,
comfortability and caution

We should just be dancing

Why aren't we dancing?

undulating like sand & ocean tides
reflecting one another
like sea & moonlight
the night is ours
together we could command the wind
& use the sun as our candle

come with me and sing
dancing across rooftops & mountain peaks
falling in harmony
like maple leaves
embracing one another
like the wind & trees,
water & reeds,
the earth & seeds

come with me
taste my kisses
obey your thirsty wishes
I promise I'm delicious
separate we're delectable dishes
together we could be a tasty meal
but I'll settle for just a touch

touch me,
we can start this dance
called a fine romance
I'll put as much time into you
as I do crafting my words
close your eyes
come with me
we have stars to burst

let's dance

haiku

You write sweet poems

on your tongue's tip. I want to

devour each line.

3 Minute Muse

your lips kiss my face when i awake
be my night-time salvation
make me a born-again freak

last night
we did naughty things
the table broke
the sun shattered
the universe quaked
when you spit that rhyme
your words
made love
to mine

the texture of your flow
reverberates through my mind
disrupting my mental stability
you don't just rock my world
you fracture it's continents
boil its seas, and provide
that chilling calm simultaneously

read that verse again
it's as if you wrapped your legs
around my mind
arousing my thoughts

read that verse again
so we can play that game
touch by word

kiss by comma
sex... period

let's compose a poem
lyric by lyric
we'll press our bodies
together between couplets
your body is my notebook
let me navigate your crevices
letting beauty marks & blemishes
punctuate my sentences
incubating romance
when you get off stage

soul eyes

when I look into your eyes

I hear Coltrane's heavenly horn

in your pupils

dreams & stars are born

haiku

The last good meal that

I had for dinner this week

was between her thighs

Wednesday, 9:45am

We did it in the kitchen
right by the stove
after you cooked me breakfast
in your underclothes
we were supposed to do the dishes
they were left to soak
we'd have done it on the table
but that cheap thang woulda broke
you kneeled on the chair
we found the right angle for the stroke
then you put your foot on the sink
next to the dish for the meatloaf
we got too tired of the counter
so we took it to the wall
made the pictures shake
plaques fell in the hall
your booty damn near left smudges in the paint
we had to crack a window so neither one of us would faint
we took it to the bedroom to put the icing on the cake
apartment pounding from the vibrations
of the break beat bass

Mood Indigo

we should just be dancing (part ii)

we should just be dancing
sadly, its not that simple
i hear objections
crashing our music like cymbals

like mirrors on pedestals
we keep up appearances
we should just be dancing
but they want the music to stop
your family says that i'm a gentlemen
my integrity can't be diminished
i'm appropriate as a friend
as a lover i'm off limits

we should just be dancing
you denied me 3 times
like Peter the day before
Jesus was crucified
i'm no martyr
being with you is harder
when i know your parents
want their daughter
to stick to her own kind
its not right
that you could be placed
in the position
to be forced to decide

they asked if we are together
you lied and said it wasn't true

you told me how hard it is to break tradition
we needed to take our time
let things gradually transition

we've practiced duets
like thieves in the night
stealing moments of passion
between moments in passing
i don't understand
why you fear them catching
onto what we are
your denials cut like knives
they leave many scars

we should just be dancing
all we seem to lack
is an appropriate stage
where we don't have to
restrict the freedom of love
what we feel for each other is rare
i'm getting tired
of playing musical chairs

we should just be dancing
not giving a fuck who cares

haiku

this love has become

the very instrument of

my crucifixion

Gambit

we had an agreement
no rules
no ties
no commitment
separate lives
just sex

this is not an arrangement advised between friends

the four letter word frequently used
went from fuck to hate to love

the dj placed his finger on the vinyl
scratched it between each randomly
sometimes hate meant love
fuck meant fuck
then fuck meant love
love meat hate
two sides of the same coin
with fuck as the serrated edge
separating the two

fate flipped the coin
it landed on its side
she fell in love
with only half of me

glimpses my whole self
came to her in spurts

we painted illusions
hid our true secrets in shame
behind fig leaves

fate tossed the coin
she called heads, i called tails
it landed somewhere in-between

its jagged edge was sharp enough
to tear the curtain of our illusions
our mistakes became visible
bitten sweet fruit left on the night table
friendships tossed between our scattered clothes

we should have known better
maybe we did

bitter sweet dreams

i taste sweet tears
in my sleep
you make me cry
sugar coated tears
you know i love my sweets
you fill my smile
with shots of lime
my joy turns sour
every half an hour
but for some reason
you hold some power
got me fallin'
like the towers
nowadays i sit
pulling
petals
off
flowers

she loves me
she loves me not
this is worth it
this is not

my stomach is tied up in knots

my heart bleeds
each time
the pen   hits the page
our love was

the sweetest love song
ever played
now the song is sung
the dance has finished
i'm tired of writing poems
the ink blurs
with every sentence

art, poetry, music
is supposedly therapeutic
but the truth is convoluted
you are both
blessed & cursed
to do this:
the word is unapologetic
generous & ruthless
those who believe they control it
learn they are foolish
you may master your craft
but you never rule it
you function as a vessel
channeling emotions and divine energy
a broken heart can transform
ambitious drive to lethargy

i sat on the floor
scrambled
poems & letters
like cowry shells
to divine our future

they formed a sentence
telling me to be still,
and no amount of wishing
can ever wish love real

Crucified Idols

I

Many a good Christian
judge other religions
like new age Pharisees
eager to repeat the crucifixion
it's a shame that in Jesus' name
Africans were chained
exported as chattel
under the same banner
Constantine's army flew in battle

I'm not waging war
against all Christians
but too many dismiss
indigenous spiritual beliefs
as pagan superstition,
heresy, blasphemy, or devil worship
not realizing these beliefs
influenced most churches

too many Blacks pray
at the foot of the cross
unaware of the cost
our ancestors paid,
or that missionaries were paid
to make us slaves

when they arrived
we had the land
they had the Bible
they stole the land
with their rifles

we were left with the Bible
we turned the other cheek
like good disciples

we were taught to believe
our ancestral traditions were primitive
and praise missionaries for saving us
from so-called savage ways
the way Christianity was brought to us
made it seem we were destined to be slaves

how can you worship God
when you revel in self-hate?
do we need 3 more nails on a cross
to set the record straight?

we live in the resurrected Roman state
activists, leaders & revolutionaries
face the same fate:
stand down, convert, snitch,
or be burned at the stake
how many of our beloved
have been crucified for our sake?
sadly all most of us do
is pray and wait
for the next coming of the One
to lead us to a brighter day

II

In my bible,
they crucified Jesus next to Ba'al
after Santa got shot up like 50
for decking the wrong halls
they put Malcom & Ché on the cross
because they could see the writing on the wall
it was the blueprint to unlock
a new Pandora's box
built to usher in Babylon's fall

in my visions
I've seen Buddha dismembered like Osiris
& the pantheon of Hindu Devas
burned in the fires

in America
we crucify the divine
letting their lifeblood flow
to feed states of mind
only the state poisons minds

only in America
would people make such graven images
President's faces on dollar bills
encircled by "In God We Trust"
revering that pale face
as the true God's bust

they crucify our idols
and call our Gods false

we need to crucify their idols
before the heavens erupt

in America we worship money
foreigners think
it's a land of milk & honey
but can't see the blood running
drained from the lynched bodies
of activists & slaves
young men & women of color
cast in early graves

they murder our idols
we resurrect them as martyrs
how many of humankind's
sons & daughters
must fall before we realize
that money is the beast
we say it's the root of all evil
yet we kneel at its feet

we won't put greed on the cross
yet we are quick to call
other people's Gods
graven images
its seems even avarice
enslaves religion

they crucify our beliefs as idols
like humans crucified God
we need to crucify the real idols
before we lose sight of love

III

Many a good Christian
judge other religions
like new age Pharisees
eager to repeat the crucifixion

atheists claim God is fiction
capitalists pray *In Greed We Trust*
Muslims say *Allah Akbar*
& that they're the only right ones
Hindus say there are many paths
but only marry those of their tradition
Buddhism has saints
but claims to not be a religion
indigenous Afrikans cosmologies vary
due to the continent's diversity,
Native American traditions barely
survived Colonial adversity
they speak of The Great Spirit
Jesus said the Word of God
is written in your heart
so don't fear it

if pious people claim
humanity is saved
only through their religion
then why has so much
blood been shed due to religion?
the intolerance is enough
to make God commit suicide
or let us kill God

like Jesus when he died
Forgive them Father...
They know not what they do...
The Great Spirit is beyond their understanding,
please give them a clue

message after message
we still haven't received the fax
like an e-mail sent to a full account
bound to bounce back

we love to dirty the spiritual
with the monetary
now I see why Jesus
overturned money changers' tables
in the sanctuary
I understand why Muslims
do no attempt to depict Allah's face
just like early Christians would consider
Roman Catholic artwork a heretic disgrace
who are we to limit the Most High
to a bearded face
when he/she/it defies time & space
knowledge and understanding

I've grown to know why Hindu Devas
have many limbs & faces
God is infinite
like the sum number of worship spaces

we need to break the chains
that keep us in stasis

follow Jesus' example
be intolerant of intolerance
love our neighbors as we love ourselves

who people pray to is their business
we need to live our prayers for a better world
let the revolution unfurl in our actions

see the greatness of God
in another's faith
worship without ego

Judge not, lest you be judged first

none of us are perfect
none of us hold all the answers
let us not be pretentious enough
to spill more blood over beliefs
to be pawns of the powerful
generators of their wealth
funding their quest to cause Armageddon

maybe
if we can be
our highest selves

we can bring   this Earth
                      just a little closer
                                to Paradise

Glossary

Disclaimer

I have defined the following terms to the best of my ability so that you can understand these terms in the context of my poetry. For more information on the items listed below, I encourage you to research them for yourselves.

Allah Akbar

an Arabaic phrase used in Islam that means "God is Great."

Amun

the name of a deity, in Egyptian cosmology usually associated with creation, royalty, the sun, and the preservation of moral principles (M'aat).

Avatar

in Hindu cosmology, an Avatar is the incarnation (bodily manifestation) of the Supreme Being (God, Vishnu) on Earth. Avatars deliberately descend to Earth for the purpose of redeeming humanity. Examples of Avatars in Hinduism would include Krishna and Rama. Some Hindus view Jesus Christ as an example of an Avatar as well.

Ba` al

originally used as a divine title for Yahweh (God) in Judaism. The title was later abandoned and associated with shame, and with false worship.

Constantine

Constantine I was the Roman Emperor who both legalized Christianity in the Roman Empire and had it adopted as the national religion. He was a lifelong pagan, and converted to Christianity on his deathbed.

Deva

a Hindu word meaning both "God" and "Goddess." Actually, the Greek and Latin words for God (Deus) are derived from this Sanskrit word.

Great Spirit

is a concept of a Supreme Being prevalent among Native American cultures. The Great Spirit is viewed as both personal and as the very fabric of reality (a trait shared with Hindu & Yoruba cosmologies).

Krishna

8th Avatar of Vishnu, and one of the most beloved Deities in Hindu cosmology.

Ogun

in Yoruba cosmology is an Orisha representing patience, hard work, discipline, dedication, perseverance, justice, level headedness, structure, and creativity. Ogun is the patron Orisha of warriors and Hunters. He is known as the Path Opener, meaning that Ogun is the force that supports one in accomplishing a decided task.

Pharisees

in Christian theology, the Pharisees were a group of self-righteous Jewish aristocrats and theologians who emphasized the following of God's rules and laws more than God's love. Jesus' teachings were in direct opposition to theirs, and in an effort to preserve their power, as Jesus' teachings were growing in popularity, they conspired with the Roman government to have him executed.

Osiris

in Egyptian comsmology, Osiris is the God of death and the ruler of the underworld. He is the judge of the dead in the afterlife. He is the husband of Isis, and was murdered and dismembered by his brother, Set.

Samsara

the cycle of birth, death, & rebirth in Hindu cosmology.

Shiva

is a form of God in Hindu cosmology, and part of the Trimutri (Hindu Trinity of Brahama, Vishnu, & Shiva).

www.ingramcontent.com/pod-product-compliance
Lightning Source LLC
Chambersburg PA
CBHW022040090426
42741CB00007B/1143